THE LONG JOHN CAFÉ

(COMPETITION VERSION)

BY
L. HENRY DOWELL

EDITED FOR COMPETITION
BY
MITZI STINSON

BLACK BOX THEATRE PUBLISHING

To order additional copies of the script, or to request performance rights, please contact us at wwwblackboxtheatrepublishing.com

ISBN #**978-0692332948**

Printed in the United States of America.

Original Competition Cast

The Bus Driver……………………………………Grant Goracke
Nixon……………………………………………Rece Vaught
Material Girl……………………………………Reagan Smith
Marion……………………………………………Will Reeson
Shirley……………………………………………Morgan Preissler
Avon Lady………………………………………Kaylee Rhoades
Nanny……………………………………………Emily Towns
The King…………………………………………Rees Lyon
Audrey……………………………………………Baylee Thiel
Norma Jeane……………………………………Reagan Janzen
The Colonel………………………………………Beau Craig
Moon Princess……………………………………Brayden Rhoades
Sun King…………………………………………Jayden Devries
Eli Dorkboy/Really-Super-Swell-Guy……….Dayne Hinrichs
Phyllis Phelps……………………………………Tristan Larson
Dr. McNasty………………………………………Sydnee Craig
Julie Childs………………………………………Chloe Craig
Jackio O……………………………………………Diandra Polt
Cher…………………………………………………Morgan Wilson
James Dean………………………………………Colton Craig
The Kings Choir…………Taylor Greathouse, Kylie Schwab,
Sydney Janzen, Hannah Preissler,
Brooke Wilson, Ariel Stithem,
Dakota Lindon, Cole Consbruck

Original Competition Crew

Director……………………………………………Mitzi Stinson
Assistant Director………………………………Bobbi Sorensen
Student Director…………………………………Lexi Preissler
Stage Manager……………………………………Alex Goracke
Crew……………………Bowdie Larson, Leslie Rodridguez,
Mary Wiles, Hannah Farrall, Rody Lyon,
Michele Gaskill, Sidney Voichahoske,
Alex Coats, Jordan Hansen, Brooke Good,
Aubrey Leichty, Courtney Hoelck,
Kendel Wilson, Dawson Bartunek

THE LONG JOHN CAFÉ

SCENE ONE

TIME: A few hours before the world ends.
PLACE: A small café located at the border of reality.

LIGHTS rise on The Long John Café. Several patrons are seated around tables making small talk. THE BUS DRIVER, NIXON and MATERIAL GIRL are sitting at one table. MARION, SHIRLEY, and AVON LADY are seated at another. NANNY and THE GOVERNATOR are playing darts. AUDREY and NORMA JEANE are waiting tables. KING is at bar, talking to THE COLONEL. MOON PRINCESS and SUN KING enter. THEY hold signs, though we don't see what is written on them.

SUN KING
Far out! This place is cool!

MOON PRINCESS
Yeah man...see what I told you.

SUN KING
Too bad it's all about to blink out of existence.

MOON PRINCESS
Yeah man. Bummer. Wanna get some coffee?

SUN KING
Absolutely.

COLONEL
Well hello there! Welcome to the Long John Café. You're just in time for the big celebration.

SUN KING
Big celebration?

COLONEL
Why yeah. Don't you know what's going on?

MOON PRINCESS
Sure…we know...but do you know?

COLONEL
Of course I know. This is my café.

SUN KING
Well, why don't you tell us what you know, and we'll tell you what we know. That way we're all on the same page.

COLONEL
What planet have you folks been on?

MOON PRINCESS
Actually...

COLONEL
This is the night that the universe's greatest hero is coming right here to my little café to make some sort of big announcement.

SUN KING
This guy sounds cool. Who is he?

COLONEL
Who is he? Why "he" is the one true champion of universal peace and justice, Really-Super-Swell-Guy!

EVERYONE

(Rising and placing THEIR hands over THEIR hearts.)

Really-Super-Swell-Guy!!!

MOON PRINCESS

Wow, I didn't see that coming.

AUDREY

There's nobody in the universe like Really-Super-Swell-Guy.

NIXON

Yeah, he's faster than a speeding Amtrak!

MARION

And he's more powerful than a Brahma bull!

MATERIAL GIRL

And he looks great in spandex!

EVERYONE looks at HER.

MATERIAL GIRL

Well, he does.

EVERYONE agrees.

SUN KING

So what's the big announcement he's gonna make?

MARION

Nobody knows for sure, but it must have something to do with the turn of the century.

MATERIAL GIRL

Isn't it exciting? The 21st Century! Who knows what great discoveries await us there?

NANNY
Maybe a cure for the common cold.

AVON LADY
Or the implementation of the four day work week.

EVERYONE looks at HER.

AVON LADY
It could happen.

BUS DRIVER
Anything's possible in the future. Look at all the great stuff that's happened over the last hundred years. The invention of TV.

NANNY
Disneyland.

KING
Rock and roll.

NIXON
Toilet paper.

EVERYONE
Yay toilet paper!

SUN KING
When is he supposed to get here?

COLONEL
Why, right about now.

EVERYONE turns toward the door. It opens. EVERYONE gasps, then sighs with disappointment as ELI DORKBOY and PHYLLIS PHELPS enter. SHE is a no-

nonsense journalist. HE is a…well, a dork. ELI has a secret though. HE is really REALLY-SUPER-SWELL-GUY.

ELI

…but Phyllis, couldn't you get someone else to help you with this particular assignment? I really have something important to do today.

PHYLLIS

Eli, do you want to be a dork all of your life? This is only "the" biggest story of the millennium. This story could put both of us on the stellar map. Where's your ambition? Wouldn't you like to win a Pulitzer?

ELI

Sure…someday, but, Phyllis, it's really, really important.

PHYLLIS

What do you have to do that's so important?

ELI

I gotta go…and…wash my socks!

PHYLLIS

You have to go wash your socks?

ELI

They're really dirty socks Phyllis.

PHYLLIS

Well they would have to be to cause you so much emotional trauma.

NORMA JEANE enters. Blonde. The kind gentlemen prefer.

NORMA JEANE
What can I get you folks?

ELI
I would like to have a...HUBBA-HUBBA-HUBBA!

NORMA JEANE
I think we're out of that, but I'll check the kitchen.

PHYLLIS
You'll have to excuse him, he's a dork.

NORMA JEANE
No problem. So, what'll it be?

ELI
Milk.

NORMA JEANE
Pardon?

ELI
I would like a glass of milk.

NORMA JEANE
Ok....Would you like a straw with that?

ELI
Oh no. I like to live life on the wild side.

NORMA JEANE
Whatever you say, Butch. How about you Miss?

PHYLLIS
Nothing for me, thanks. I'm working.

NORMA JEANE
You guys are reporters, right?

PHYLLIS

Yes, I'm Phyllis Phelps and this is my appropriately named cameraman, Eli Dorkboy. We're reporters for the Daily Cosmos. We're going to cover the big announcement tonight.

NORMA JEANE

It's all very exciting isn't it? The world's greatest hero right here in our little café. It's enough to make a girl giddy.

PHYLLIS

So you consider yourself a fan of Really-Super-Swell-Guy…Miss…?

NORMA JEANE

Norma Jeane. And yes, I'm his biggest fan. It's not very often a girl gets to meet a real honest to goodness superhero face to face.

(Looks at HER watch.)

Holy hole in a doughnut! Look at the time! That intergalactic stud will be here any minute and look at me! I gotta go get ready!

NORMA JEANE exits running.

PHYLLIS

Did you see that Eli?

ELI

I sure did. I think she has the hots for Really-Super-Swell-Guy!

PHYLLIS

Can I confide something in you Eli?

PHYLLIS

I'm actually here to expose Really-Super-Swell-Guy for the fraud that he is.

ELI

(Nervous.)

F...fr...fraud?!?! Why, whatever do you mean by that Phyllis?

PHYLLIS

Look. I'm not saying that the stuff this guy has accomplished is all bogus. There are plenty of eyewitness accounts of his "good deeds". He's a super person right? That's what they do. Good deeds. I'm sure his heart is in the right place. But come on. Nobody could be that fantastic. He must have some dirty laundry lying around somewhere.

ELI

But Phyllis, with all the good this guy has done, why would you want to dig up dirt on him?

PHYLLIS

Eli. That's what we reporters do. That's what people want. Deep dark secrets sell papers by the millions and make Pulitzer Prize winners out of the messengers. That's you and me, Eli.

ELI

That's not very nice Phyllis.

PHYLLIS

It's not a very nice world Eli.

ELI

Maybe that's why we need a guy like Really-Super-Swell-Guy then. To right the wrongs. To give people hope.

ELI

Doesn't he impress you at all?

PHYLLIS

Impress me? Oh, I'm impressed by his rugged good looks. Sure. His keen fashion sense. Certainly. But he isn't real, Eli. He isn't real at all.

ELI

What are we doing here if he isn't real?

ELI slips off during the next speech.

PHYLLIS

Oh, he exists. But how could a woman get so giddy over a grown man running around in his underwear? A "hero"? What's that anyway? The history books are full of so-called heroes. Men like George Washington, Davy Crocket, M. C. Hammer. And none of them pranced around in outlandish outfits like high priced circus clowns. They were real guys who overcame great obstacles to become heroes. These days any bozo with a cape and a cool gimmick can call himself a hero. They're everywhere. Movies, TV, books, magazines...heck, there is a guy across the street at the convenience store who calls himself Captain Clerk. I mean, really! Just because a guy can leap skyscrapers, bend steel with his bare hands, and outrun an Amtrak doesn't automatically make him a hero!

ELI has entered. HE is dressed in HIS superhero costume, and strikes a heroic pose. NO ONE seems to notice though. HE realizes HE is still wearing HIS glasses. HE removes them, again striking a heroic pose, and EVERYONE notices, except PHYLLIS.

PHYLLIS

I can't wait till he gets here so I can tell him exactly what I think of him.

REALLY

I'm here.

PHYLLIS turns, sees HIM, and then faints.

AUDREY

Are you him? Really-Super-Swell-Guy?

REALLY

I hope so. I'm wearing his underwear.

AVON LADY

My hero!

SHIRLEY

Oh my goodness!

REALLY

Does anyone have any smelling salts?

COLONEL

I do sir!

COLONEL gets the bottle from behind the bar. REALLY places it under PHYLLIS' nose. SHE stirs.

REALLY

Are you alright Phyllis?

PHYLLIS

Yes, I'm fine. Wait...how did you know my name?

REALLY

I'm Really-Super-Swell-Guy. I know everything.

MARION

What a guy!

BUS DRIVER
You're telling me!

PHYLLIS makes it to HER feet. ALL LADIES crowd around REALLY and give HIM a kiss on the cheek. After kiss EACH says "Tee-hee".

PHYLLIS
Ok. Ok. Break it up.

REALLY
Are you sure you're ok, Miss Phelps?

PHYLLIS
I'm fine. Thanks.

REALLY
All in a day's work. Now, if it's ok, I have a very important announcement I need to make.

EVERYONE gathers around.

PHYLLIS
(Looking around.)
Wait a minute...where did Eli go?

REALLY
Eli? Who's Eli? Is he your boyfriend or something?

PHYLLIS
Eli? Oh no. Yuck. No way…are you kidding me? Eeeeeeeewwwww...no, he's my partner. Sort of. You wouldn't like him. He's a real dork.

REALLY
Yes. You're probably right. I hate dorks.

NIXON
Yeah. Me too.

PHYLLIS
Will you grant me an interview Really-Super-Swell-Guy?

REALLY
Please just call me by my nickname.

PHYLLIS
And what's that?

REALLY
"Really".

PHYLLIS
"Really"? Really?

REALLY
Really. "Really".

PHYLLIS
Interesting. Now what about that interview?

REALLY
Of course. Anything for you Phyllis.

PHYLLIS
Who would you consider to be your greatest nemesis?

REALLY
Tooth decay.

PHYLLIS
Tooth decay?

BUS DRIVER
I know I hate it.

PHYLLIS
What about Dr. McNasty?

REALLY
What about her?

PHYLLIS
I think all of these people would like to know who she really is. Am I right folks?

MATERIAL GIRL
I want to know!

NANNY
Me too!

PHYLLIS
Will you give us the lowdown, Really? Tell us about Dr. McNasty. Inquiring minds want to know.

REALLY
Very well, Dr. McNasty may be the most intelligent human being on Earth, as well as one of the moodiest. For years, she tried to defeat me with one crazy scheme after another, none of them successful....obviously, because here I am. Anyway, after our last encounter she simply disappeared.

PHYLLIS
Have we seen the last of her?

REALLY
I'd like to think so.

EVERYONE agrees.

REALLY
The last time we met was in 1997. She was attempting to steal every existing copy of Austin Powers: International Man of Mystery.

NIXON
Every copy...why that would be...

REALLY
Yes. It was an ambitious plan.

AVON LADY
But why? It's not even that great of a movie.

EVERYONE agrees.

PHYLLIS
And you haven't seen her since?

REALLY
Neither hide nor hair.

SHIRLEY
Oh my goodness!

PHYLLIS
Ok. Enough chit chat. Let me ask you some real questions. What's your favorite color?

REALLY
Red, white and blue.

PHYLLIS
Very patriotic. Your favorite song?

REALLY
The Star Spangled Banner.

PHYLLIS

Your favorite food?

REALLY

Apple pie, of course.

PHYLLIS

Of course, and I bet you love your mother?

REALLY

Immensely.

PHYLLIS

What color underwear am I wearing?

REALLY

Purple.

PHYLLIS

Your favorite movie?

REALLY

The Little Mermaid.

PHYLLIS

Really?

REALLY

Hey, would I lie?

PHYLLIS

So, who are you, really?

REALLY

Eli…..I…I…I…don’t remember my real name. You see, my parents were aliens from a far away galaxy. Our ship crash landed here when I was very young. I was the only survivor.

EVERYONE is crying, even the GOVERNATOR.

COLONEL
That is such a sad story.

REALLY
Yes...it is...but even though the blood that flows through these veins is from a place that's far, far away from here, I still consider myself to be one of you. A real American. I was found by a kindly old couple who took me in. Fed me three square meals a day, worked me 40 hours a week at minimum wage, took a third of it in taxes, and then laughed at me when I couldn't afford designer jeans.

AVON LADY
He is a real American.

REALLY
Yes. I am. And I'm just as normal as anybody here, except that Hippy over there...what's his deal?

SUN KING
Peace, man.

EVERYONE applauds.

PHYLLIS
That was amazing. You really have a way with words.

REALLY
Phyllis, words are the greatest of all superpowers. They have the ability to transport us to untold worlds at any time of our choosing.

PHYLLIS
You should have been a poet.

REALLY
That was my second career choice.

Phone rings. COLONEL answers it.

COLONEL
Hello? Thank you for calling The Long John Café. What can I do for you? What? WHAT? WHAT???
(Hands phone to REALLY.)
It's for you Really-Super-Swell-Guy.

REALLY
Hello? Yes, this is Really-Super-Swell-Guy speaking. What can I do for you? What? WHAT? WHAT??? Oh no! I'll be right there!
(Hangs up.)
I have to go. There is an emergency situation which requires my immediate attention!

HE runs to the door and exits. EVERYONE follows. THEY all look up to indicate that HE is flying away.

EVERYONE
Ooooh...aaaah...wow...etc.

PHYLLIS
What was that all about?

COLONEL
That poor woman. Her pet cat Fluffy is stuck up in a tree.

PHYLLIS
He left to get someone's cat out of a tree?

COLONEL
That's a real hero for you ma'am. No job too big, no job too small.

PHYLLIS
He didn't even get around to making his big announcement.

NORMA JEANE enters. Gussied up.

NORMA JEANE
Ok. Here I am. Hey, where is he?

PHYLLIS
You just missed him.

NORMA JEANE
What? Are you kidding me? Did he leave a tip?

PHYLLIS
Nope.

NORMA JEANE
Shucks.

SHE exits again. EVERYONE has returned to THEIR seats. NANNY and THE GOVERNATOR are playing darts.

NANNY
Did you see the way he just took off into the sky? And no umbrella.

AVON LADY
Very impressive.

NANNY
Not as impressive as that dart grouping. Good job.

AVON LADY

Lawn darts. I'm telling you; in the 21st century they are going to be the next big thing. I sold all my Microsoft stock and just bought a million shares in a big lawn dart manufacturing company.

MARION

I tell ya what, that was a real bold move there Pilgrim. It took true grit.

SHIRLEY

Oh my goodness!

AVON LADY

Can I ask you something, Shirley?

SHIRLEY

Surely.

AVON LADY

Why do you say that all the time?

SHIRLEY

What?

AVON LADY

"Oh my goodness." You say that all the time.

MARION

Yeah, I was wondering about that myself. It's kind of annoying to tell ya the truth little missy.

SHIRLEY

People think it's cute.

AVON LADY

What people?

SHIRLEY
You know. The audience.

AVON LADY
But, there's no audience here.

SHIRLEY
Oh...isn't there?

PAUSE.

BUS DRIVER
...so then I told her, one of these days Alice...POW! Right to the moon!

MATERIAL GIRL
And how did she respond to that?

BUS DRIVER
Not so well. She made me sleep on the couch.

MATERIAL GIRL
Women like a sensitive man.

NIXON
Really? I've been going about this all wrong then. A sensitive man, you say?

MATERIAL GIRL
Absolutely. That or give her expensive gifts. We are living in a material world after all.

BUS DRIVER
So I should buy her jewelry?

MATERIAL GIRL
Sounds like a plan to me.

AUDREY enters with drinks.

AUDREY
The rain in Spain stays mainly in the plain...the rain in Spain stays mainly in the plain...

SHE exits.

KING
(At the bar.)
What's the deal with her?

COLONEL
She's practicing her diction. She wants to be a lady.

MOON PRINCESS
This is really a great place you have here.

SUN KING
Great bunch of characters. Very "eclectic".

COLONEL
This is a special night. It's the end of the 20th century, so all of these "characters", as you call them, have come to celebrate the beginning of tomorrow. Look around you. These folks represent some of the best of what was.

BUS DRIVER
Say King...how's about a little entertainment?

KING
Well...

EVERYONE
Yeah! Come on! Let's hear it! Etc!

KING
Well, I hate to disappoint my fans!

EVERYONE

YAY!

KING grabs a guitar.

KING

Now this here is a song I wrote about a place that's near and dear to my heart. I hope you like it.

MUSIC: THE LONG JOHN CAFÉ.

KING

You know where to find me,
When the world's turned a deaf ear.
When I need some company,
Baby you'll find me here.

Long John Café!
Where I like to play!
Long John Café!
Where I go to stay!

Where friends are really friends,
And the good times never end,
Ain't no way!

EVERYONE

Ain't no way!

KING

Ain't no way!

EVERYONE

Just wait and see!

KING

Just wait and see!

EVERYONE
Just wait and see!

EVERYONE returns to THEIR original positions.

AVON LADY
You know what I like best about this place?

COLONEL
What's that?

AVON LADY
Except for an occasional lapse into song, it's really quiet and peaceful around here.

DR. MCNASTY enters, crosses down center. SHE is dressed like a mad scientist. SHE is also a very moody individual.

DR. MCNASTY
Everybody freeze!

EVERYONE shivers with gusto.

DR. MCNASTY
You people are way too literal. Now cut that out! Pay attention to me!

BUS DRIVER
Why?

DR. MCNASTY
Because I am the evil Dr. McMasty!

BUS DRIVER
Who?

DR. MCNASTY
You mean you've never heard of me?

MARION
You're some kind of movie villain, right?

DR. MCNASTY
No! I am not some kind of movie villain! I am a real villain! I'm the one all those Hollywood types base their characters on! I am the original! The one and only evil Dr. McNasty! Come on...you know me...don't you?

BUS DRIVER shrugs.

DR. MCNASTY
The scourge of goodness! Raspberry seed in the wisdom tooth of justice.
(Looks at THEM.)
Nothing?

PHYLLIS
Of course we know who you are Dr. McNasty.

DR. MCNASTY
Thank goodness. You know, there was a time when a would-be world conquering villain could get a little respect.

COLONEL
Look...Miss...?

DR. MCNASTY
Please, call me...Dr. McNasty!!!

COLONEL
Ok...Dr. McNasty!!! This is The Long John Café. This is a place where you can be yourself. Whatever that means.

DR. MCNASTY

But it isn't that simple. I am a mad genius. A villain. I studied for years to be a psychopath.

AUDREY

Then be a psychopath. Be the best psychopath anyone ever saw!

EVERYONE

Yeah!

COLONEL

That's why I opened this café. So the icons of the 20th century could come in here, kick back and be themselves. You can do anything you want to do!

NORMA JEANE

What do you want to do?

DR. MCNASTY

Well...To be quite honest, I want to conquer the world.

COLONEL

Then by golly, do it!

EVERYONE

Yeah!

DR. MCNASTY

(Whining.)

But it's so hard!

NIXON

Then you've got to come up with a full proof plan.

DR. MCNASTY

Yes...wait...how do you know so much about it? Are you a world conquering villain?

NIXON
That was my second career choice.

COLONEL
Why did you come here today?

DR. MCNASTY
It doesn't matter.

NORMA JEANE
It must have had something to do with Really-Super-Swell-Guy.

DR. MCNASTY
Of course it did.

NIXON
You must have had some diabolical scheme in mind.

DR. MCNASTY
What self-respecting villain wouldn't?

PHYLLIS
What was it?

DR. MCNASTY
I was going to expose his true identity to the world.

NIXON
Great plan!

PHYLLIS
Wait a minute! How were you planning on doing that?

DR. MCNASTY
Wait...I know you. I know I know you. But where do I know you from?

NIXON
She's that snoopy reporter, Phyllis Phelps.

DR. MCNASTY
You're that snoopy reporter, Phyllis Phelps aren't you?

NIXON
I just said that.

DR. MCNASTY
(To NIXON.)
Shhhhhhhh...
(To PHYLLIS.)
Well, aren't you?

PHYLLIS
Well, I hope so. I'm wearing her underwear.

DR. MCNASTY
To answer your question Miss Phelps, I was going to threaten to destroy this place and everyone in it if he didn't expose himself.

EVERYONE giggles a little at the "expose himself" line.

PHYLLIS
And what if he didn't...expose himself?
(Starts to giggle. Contains it.)

DR. MCNASTY
(Pulls cartoonish bomb out of bag.)
Then I will detonate this bomb!

PHYLLIS
Bomb?

NORMA JEANE

Bomb?

EVERYONE

Bomb?

DR. MCNASTY

Yes, a bomb! A bomb that I will detonate with my handy dandy detonator located right here on my wrist, should Really-Super-Swell-Guy refuse to (snicker) expose himself.

MARION

Hey pardner, he ain't here anymore. He left awhile ago.

DR. MCNASTY

What? Where did he go?

PHYLLIS

If you must know, he flew off to perform some magnificent rescue!

DR. MCNASTY

Rescue? Oh...He's gone to get someone's cat out of a tree you mean.

PHYLLIS

Uh...it doesn't matter. He's not here. And you'd better go back to wherever it was you came from before he gets back.

DR. MCNASTY

Wait! He's coming back?

PHYLLIS

Ah poop. Me and my big mouth.

DR. MCNASTY

Well in that case, I'll just wait for him.

PHYLLIS

He might be awhile.

DR. MCNASTY

That's alright. I've waited years for my opportunity to finally destroy that…Do-Nicey-Things-er! I think I can wait a little longer…uh-oh!

PHYLLIS

What's wrong?

DR. MCNASTY

I feel an evil laugh coming on! Yes... yes... here it comes... heh... heh...heh...ha-ha-ha-ha-ha... BWAH-HA-HA-HA-HA!

NIXON

Very nice.

PHYLLIS

(Looking out the window.)

Where are you when we need you Really-Super-Swell-Guy?

ELI

(Entering from bathroom.)

Here I am.

EVERYONE turns thinking it's REALLY, but seeing it's only ELI, THEY collectively sigh in disappointment.

ELI

Were you looking for me?

PHYLLIS

Not exactly Eli.

ELI

Where is Really-Super-Swell-Guy?

DR. MCNASTY
Well, he's not here, that's for certain.

ELI
(Suddenly realizing.)
Great oogly-moogly! You're the evil Dr. MCNASTY!

DR.MCNASTY
I hope so. I'm wearing his undergarments.

ELI
(Realizing that DR. MCNASTY doesn't recognize HIM.)
Oh...hi there. My name is Eli Dorkboy.
(Extends HIS hand.)
It's nice to meet you.

DR. MCNASTY
(Ignoring it.)
Not really. Where was I?

NIXON
We were waiting on Really-Super-Swell-Guy, and you were going to expose his true identity by threatening to blow us all to smithereens with your bomb.

EVERYONE looks at HIM severely.

NIXON
I was taking notes.

MARION
(To NIXON.)
You are way too into this pardner!

ELI
Did he just say bomb? I...uh...gotta go to the bathroom.

PHYLLIS

You were just in the bathroom!

BUS DRIVER

Yeah, you must have a bad case of the runs 'eh buddy?

EVERYONE

EEEEEEEEEEEEEEEEEWWWWWWWWWWWWWW!!!

PHYLLIS

You are truly an evil person, Dr. McNasty!

DR. MCNASTY

Yes. Yes I am.

ELI

I really gotta go to the bathroom Phyllis!

PHYLLIS

Will you shut up!

ELI

But I...

EVERYONE

SHUT UP!!!

PHYLLIS

Be a man for once in your life Eli. Get a spine! If people like you would learn to take care of things yourself, we wouldn't have to rely on super people all the time!

ELI

But...

DR. MCNASTY
Enough of this! Everyone sit down. I want all of you where I can see you. If anybody makes a move I'll detonate the bomb with my handy dandy wrist detonator.

KING
Hey man! That looks like a common, ordinary wristwatch to me!

DR. MCNASTY
Ah, you are perceptive Sir! As well as a snappy dresser I might add.

KING
Thank you. Thank you very much.

DR. MCNASTY
Now sit down. Everybody. We'll wait all night if we have to.

COLONEL hangs a closed sign. LIGHTS fade on all except DR. MCNASTY.

DR. MCNASTY
(Pacing back and forth.)
Where is he? Where is that moron? I'm losing my patience!

SHE exits. LIGHTS rise on others.

AVON LADY, NORMA JEANE, KING, MATERIAL GIRL. KING and COLONEL are sitting at the bar.

KING
How'd you get into this crazy business, Colonel?

COLONEL
Funny story. I originally wanted to be a chicken farmer. Till the bottom fell out.

AVON LADY

Business went bad did it?

COLONEL

Oh no. The bottom fell out of my chicken coop. Right down into a big old sinkhole.

KING

Tough luck man.

COLONEL

I took the insurance money and opened the Long John Café.

MOON PRINCESS

(Joining the conversation.)

We love this place.

SUN KING

There aren't enough places where you can just be yourself in this world.

COLONEL

Anyone is welcome here, regardless of their race, creed, color or species. You can be yourself…or someone else if you choose.

NANNY, MARION, THE GOVERNATOR and NIXON are seated at a table.

NIXON

(To MARION.)

Are you kidding me?

MARION

Not at all.

NIXON

But you're such a manly guy!

MARION

Thanks...I think.

NANNY

It's unusual for a cowboy, that's for certain. You don't mind people knowing?

MARION

Not at all. You are who you are after all.

NIXON

Well, you're a heck of a man, Marion.

NANNY

A cowboy named Marion.

MARION

That's what my mama named me.

DR. MCNASTY

(SHE has exited and re-entered with a pizza.)

Ladies and Gentlemen! May I have your attention?

EVERYONE

No.

DR. MCNASTY

Well, who cares what you say. Using my superior intellect, I have come to a conclusion. I have deduced that one of you people must in fact be Really-Super-Swell-Guy!

EVERYONE looks at EACH OTHER. ELI looks nervous.

PHYLLIS

(Amused.)

And just how did you come to this conclusion, may I ask?

DR. MCNASTY

By deduction, careful evaluation, keen assessment of all available information... and they just delivered a pizza in his name!

ELI

(To audience.)

Ah poop.

DR. MCNASTY

Now, which one of you is it?

ELI

Not me.

DR. MCNASTY

Really-Super-Swell-Guy is a hero type. All hero types love attention. So he would have to be someone with a really glamorous job!

(Points to NIXON.)

You. You are Really-Super-Swell-Guy!

NIXON

Me? But I'm your biggest fan!

DR. MCNASTY

All a ruse to throw me off the scent I'm sure. Get over against the wall so I can keep an eye on you.

NIXON moves to wall.

DR. MCNASTY

On the other hand, Really-Super-Swell-Guy has an affection for outlandish attire.

(Points to KING.)

You. You must be Really-Super-Swell-Guy.

KING

Me?

NIXON

What about me? I thought you thought I was Really-Super-Swell-Guy.

DR. MCNASTY

You are!

KING

Then who am I?

DR. MCNASTY

Really-Super-Swell-Guy!

NIXON

I'm confused.

KING

I'm all shook up!

EVERYONE

Uh huh!

DR. MCNASTY

(To KING.)

Against the wall.

KING

Ok Baby.

DR. MCNASTY

I also know that he is a man who enjoys power.

(Points at COLONEL.)

You.

(COLONEL moves to wall.)

He is also a master of disguise, so you, you, you, you, you and you.

(SHE points at AVON LADY, NORMA JEANE, AUDREY, SHIRLEY, MATERIAL GIRL, NANNY and MOON PRINCESS. ALL of THEM move to wall.)

MATERIAL GIRL

Do I look like a man to you?

DR. MCNASTY

In some of your early videos, yes.

MATERIAL GIRL

Well! I never!

DR. MCNASTY

I doubt that. Now, he thinks of himself as tough, no doubt, so you, you, you, you, and you!

(SHE has pointed at PHYLLIS, MARION, SUN KING, BUS DRIVER and THE GOVERNATOR. ALL move to the wall, leaving only ELI.)

Now one of you people is in reality, Really-Super-Swell-Guy!

PHYLLIS

This is absurd.

ELI

Yeah, what makes you thinks it has to be one of them? Maybe I'm Really-Super-Swell-Guy?

THEY ALL burst into laughter.

DR. MCNASTY

Please. My dear little man. Never in a million years would I ever consider that someone so plain and patently un-super as yourself could be the champion of goodness, Really-Super-Swell-Guy! I mean, come on!

ELI

Yes, but wouldn't a super-hero want his secret identity to be as drastically different from his costumed persona as possible?

THE CROWD ponders this.

AVON LADY

(To DR. MCNASTY.)

If I might interject, Sir....

DR. MCNASTY

Sure. Be my guest.

AVON LADY

It would seem that this unimpressive young man makes a good point.

DR. MCNASTY

Look. Who's the psychopathic mad genius here anyway? You or me?

AVON LADY

You are.

DR. MCNASTY

That's right. So back off! Now, if Mr. Hero wants to step forward, now is the time.

ELI

Ok. I'm him.

EVERYONE

WHAT???

DR. MCNASTY

You are?

PHYLLIS

Eli, don't be stupid!

ELI

No. I'm really him. I'm Really-Super-Swell-Guy.

DR. MCNASTY

OK. Prove it.

ELI

I can't.

DR. MCNASTY

So you aren't really, Really-Super-Swell-Guy after all are you?

ELI

It depends.

DR. MCNASTY

It depends on what?

ELI

On what you believe a hero should be.

(LIGHTS fade to a single spotlight.)

What makes a person a hero? A real hero. Is it a heroic name or a fancy pair of long johns? No, I don't think so. It's someone who'll go that extra mile for someone else. That person who takes your phone call when you need help and says, "Don't worry. I'll be right there." You don't have to be rocketed from some alien world or be struck by lightning, or have a cave full of crime fighting gadgets. Heroes are people we look up to every day. The common man...and woman. It's the way they carry themselves, they way they live their lives. They're bus drivers, farmers, teachers and short order cooks. They're real people. People like you and me. Yes, my name is Eli Dorkboy and maybe I'm not some powerful superperson...or maybe I am... but regardless of that, I'm here right now, and I'm willing to stand up to this villain.

EVERYONE applauds. LIGHTS back up.

DR. MCNASTY

Wonderful speech. But answer me this...hero. If the common man is as good and heroic as you claim he is, why do so many go hungry in the world? Why do we have war? Why can't we seem to take care of our own people? The common man? He couldn't care less. It's easy to stand there in the spotlight and talk about how we can change the world, but it's another thing entirely to take arms against a sea of troubles and by opposing end them. We've been here for hours and not one of you, little people, has lifted a finger to stop me.

AVON LADY

Then maybe we will. Right now.

SHE steps forward. Slowly EVERYONE ELSE takes a step forward.

DR, MCNASTY

Well, well, well. You are all finally showing some backbone. But it will do you little good when I press the detonator button on my wrist here! You don't think I'll do it but I will, I will! BWAH-HA-HA-HA-HA-HA!

(SHE pushes button. THEY cower in fear. Nothing.)

Well. What do you know?

PHYLLIS

What?

DR. MCNASTY

It is a regular wristwatch. I must have left my detonator in my other pants.

EVERYONE except PHYLLIS storms HER forcing HER to exit. ELI and PHYLLIS meet at center stage.

ELI

Well Phyllis, another day, another dollar.

PHYLLIS

You don't fool me, Eli Dorkboy.

ELI

Why, whatever do you mean Phyllis?

PHYLLIS

You are him, aren't you?

ELI

I have no idea what you're talking about.

PHYLLIS

(Putting HER finger to HIS lips.)

Shhhh. I didn't know for sure until you made that little speech. Then I was certain. You are a hero, Eli. You're my hero.

(SHE kisses HIM like no woman has ever kissed a man before.)

Let's get out of here.

THEY turn to leave, and just as THEY get to the exit, PHYLLIS turns to HIM.

PHYLLIS

Oh yeah. What was the big announcement you were supposed to make anyway?

ELI

Hmmm? Oh yeah. I found out a giant asteroid was coming this way and was going to wipe everything out of existence...

(Looks at watch.)

...right about…now.

THEY exchange a look, then look out above the audience as the sound of something big approaching is heard.

ELI

Ah poop.

The sound gets closer and louder, as the lights get brighter and brighter and brighter and brighter until SUDDEN BLACKOUT!

THE END (OF THE WORLD AS WE KNOW IT.)

Thank you for purchasing and reading this play. If you enjoyed it, we'd appreciate a review on Amazon.com.

On the following pages you will find a selection of other plays from the Black Box Theatre Publishing Company catalog presented for you at no additional cost.

Enjoy!!!

NOW AVAILABLE!!!

WANTED: SANTA CLAUS is the story of what happens when a group of department store moguls decide to replace Santa Claus with the shiny new "KRINGLE 3000", codenamed...ROBO-SANTA! Now it's up to Santa's elves to save the day! But Santa's in no shape to take on his stainless steel counterpart! He'll have to train for his big comeback. Enter Mickey, one of the toughest elves of all time! He'll get Santa ready for the big showdown! But it's going to mean reaching deep down inside to find "the eye of the reindeer"!

Cast Size 23 Flexible M-F Roles Doubling Possible.

Royalties: $50.00 per performance.

Running Time: Approximately 90 Minutes.

NOW AVAILABLE!!!

At the edge of the universe sits The Long John Cafe. A place where the average guy and the average "Super" guy can sit and have a cup of coffee and just be themselves...or, someone else if that's what they want. The cafe is populated by iconic figures of the 20th Century, including cowboys, hippies, super heroes and movie stars. They've come to celebrate the end of the old Century and the beginning of tomorrow! That is, if they make it through the night! It seems the evil Dr. MCNASTY has other plans for our heroes. Like their total destruction!

Cast Size: 17 9M 8F.

Royalties: $50.00 per performance.

Running Time: Approximately 90 Minutes.

NOW AVAILABLE!!!

Jacklyn Sparrow and the Lady Pirates of the Caribbean is our brand new swashbuckling pirate parody complete with bloodthirsty buccaneers in massive sword clanking battle scenes!! A giant wise cracking parrot named Polly!! Crazy obsessions with eye liner!! And just who is Robert, the Dreaded Phylum Porifera!!!

Please Note: We offer large and small cast versions of this play. Cast and royalty numbers for both are below.

Cast Size: 45/13 Flexible M-F Roles Doubling Possible.

Royalties: $50.00 per performance.

Running Time: Approximately120/45 Minutes.

NOW AVAILABLE!!!

"May the Dwarf be with you in this wacky take on the classic fairy tale which will have audiences rolling in the floor with laughter!

What happens when you mix an articulate mirror, a conceited queen, a prince dressed in purple, seven little people with personality issues, a basket of kumquats and a little Star Wars for good measure?

Cast Size: 12 Flexible M-F Roles.

Royalty: $50.00 per performance.

Running Time: Approximately 45 Minutes.

NOW AVAILABLE!!!

Even Adam

In the beginning, there was a man.
Then there was a woman.
And then there was this piece of fruit...
...and that's when everything went horribly wrong!
Even Adam is a short comedy exploring the relationship between men and women right from day one.

Why doesn't he ever bring her flowers like he used to?
Why doesn't she laugh at his jokes anymore?
And just who is that guy in the red suit?
And how did she convince him to eat that fruit, anyway?

Cast Size: 3 2M-1F.

Royalties: $35.00 per performance.

Running Time: Approximately 10 Minutes.

NOW AVAILABLE!!!

THE FOUR PRESIDENTS is an educational play which examines the lives and characters of four of the most colorful personalities to hold the office. George Washington, Abraham Lincoln, Theodore Roosevelt and Richard Nixon. Much of the dialogue comes from the Presidents' own words.

A perfect show for schools!

Cast Size: 10 Flexible M-F Roles with Doubling Possible.

Royalties: $50.00 per performance.

Running Time: Approximately 60 Minutes.

NOW AVAILABLE!!!

The lights rise on a beautiful sunset.
A mermaid is silhouetted against an ocean backdrop.
Hauntingly familiar music fills the air.
Then...the Lawyer shows up.
And that's when the fun really begins!

It's The Little Mermaid (More or Less.)

Cast Size: 30 Flexible M-F Roles with Doubling Possible.

Royalties: $50.00 per performance.

Running Time: Approximately 45 Minutes.

NOW AVAILABLE!!!

Shorespeare is loosely based on a Midsummer Night's Dream. Shakespeare, with the help of Cupid, has landed at the Jersey Shore. Cupid inspires him to write a play about two New Jersey sweethearts, Cleo and Toni. Shakespeare is put off by their accent and way of talking, but decides to send the two teenagers on a course of true love. Toni and Cleo are determined to get married right after they graduate from high school, but in order to do so they must pass this course of true love that Cupid's pixies create and manipulate. As they travel along the boardwalk at the Jersey Shore, Cleo and Toni, meet a handful of historical figures disguised as the carnies. Confucius teaches Cleo the "Zen of Snoring", Charles Ponzi teaches them the importance of "White Lies", Leonardo Da Vinci shows them the "Art of Multitasking", and finally they meet Napolean who tries to help them to "Accept Shortcomings" of each other. After going through all these lessons, the sweethearts decide that marriage should wait, and Cupid is proud of Shakespeare who has finally reached out to the modern youth.

NOW AVAILABLE!!!

Everyone has heard the phrase, "it's the squeaky wheel that gets the oil," but how many people know the Back-story? The story begins in a kingdom far, far away over the rainbow – a kingdom called Spokend. This kingdom of wheels is a happy one for the gods have blessed the tiny hamlet with plentiful sunshine, water and most important –oil. Until a terrible drought starts to dry up all the oil supplies. What is to be done?

The powerful barons of industry and politicians decide to hold a meeting to decide how to solve the situation. Since Spokend is a democracy all the citizens come to the meeting but their voices are ignored – especially the voice of one of the poorer citizens of the community suffering from a squeak that can only be cured with oil, Spare Wheel and his wife Fifth Wheel. Despite Spare Wheel's desperate pleas for oil, he is ignored and sent home without any help or consideration.

Without oil, Spare Wheel's squeak becomes so bad he loses his job and his family starts to suffer when his sick leave and unemployment benefits run out. What is he to do? Spare Wheel and Fifth Wheel develop a scheme that uses the squeak to their advantage against the town magistrate Big Wheel who finally relents and gives over the oil. Thus, for years after in the town of Spokend citizens in need of help are told "It's the squeaky wheel that gets the oil."

NOW AVAILABLE!!!

Once upon a time, a beautiful princess was placed under a magic spell by an evil fairy. A spell that would cause her to fall into a deep, deep sleep. A sleep from which she would awaken 1000 years later.

It's "Sleeping Beauty meets Buck Rogers" in this play for young audiences.

Royalties: $50.00 per performance.

Cast Size: 13 with flexible extras.

Running Time: Approximately 45 minutes.

NOW AVAILABLE!!!

Santa Claus. Frosty. Rudolph. Jack Frost.

This Christmas…if you've got a problem and if you can find them then maybe you can hire…THE SLEIGH TEAM!!!

The team is hired by lowly clerk, Bob Crachit to help his boss, the miserly old Ebenezer Scrooge find a little "Christmas Spirit"!

Royalties: $50.00 per performance.

Cast Size: 6

Running Time: Approximately 45 minutes.

NOW AVAILABLE!!!

The Odd Princesses is a parody/mash-up that opens with a group of princesses assembled for a card game in the palace of the notoriously messy Snow White. Late to arrive to the party is the perpetually neat Cinderella who has run away from home after becoming fed up with being treated like a maid by her stepmother. With no where else to turn, the two total opposites decide to move in together! What could go wrong?

Royalties: $50.00 per performance.

Cast Size: 8 with extras possible.

Running Time: Approximately 45 minutes.

Made in the USA
Las Vegas, NV
08 February 2024

85482422R10039